WITHDRAWN

WEEKLY WR READER®
EARLY LEARNING LIBRARY

LET'S READ
ABOUT
Animals

Crocodiles

by Kathleen Pohl

Reading consultant: Susan Nations, M.Ed.,
author/literacy coach/consultant
in literacy development

Please visit our web site at: www.garethstevens.com
For a free color catalog describing Weekly Reader® Early Learning Library's list
of high-quality books, call 1-877-445-5824 (USA) or 1-800-387-3178 (Canada).
Weekly Reader® Early Learning Library's fax: (414) 336-0164.

Library of Congress Cataloging-in-Publication Data

Pohl, Kathleen.
   Crocodiles / by Kathleen Pohl.
     p. cm. — (Let's read about animals)
   Includes bibliographical references and index.
   ISBN-13: 978-0-8368-7815-8 (lib. bdg.)
   ISBN-13: 978-0-8368-7822-6 (softcover)
   1. Crocodiles—Juvenile literature. I. Title.
   QL666.C925P64   2007
   597.98'2—dc22   2006030453

This edition first published in 2007 by
Weekly Reader® Early Learning Library
A Member of the WRC Media Family of Companies
330 West Olive Street, Suite 100
Milwaukee, WI 53212 USA

Copyright © 2007 by Weekly Reader® Early Learning Library

Editor: Dorothy L. Gibbs
Art Direction: Tammy West
Cover design and page layout: Kami Strunsee
Picture research: Diane Laska-Swanke

Picture credits: Cover, title © Philippa Lawson/naturepl.com; p. 5 © Toby Sinclair/naturepl.com;
pp. 6-7 Kami Strunsee/© Weekly Reader® Early Learning Library; p. 9 © Pete Oxford/naturepl.com;
p. 11 © Frank Woerle/Auscape; pp. 13, 21 © Anup Shah/naturepl.com; p. 15 © Lynn Cropp/Auscape;
p. 17 © Fritz Polking/Auscape; p. 19 © Jan Aldenhoven/Auscape

Printed in the United States of America

1 2 3 4 5 6 7 8 9 10 10 09 08 07 06

Note to Educators and Parents

Reading is such an exciting adventure for young children! They are beginning to integrate their oral language skills with written language. To encourage children along the path to early literacy, books must be colorful, engaging, and interesting; they should invite the young reader to explore both the print and the pictures.

The *Let's Read About Animals* series is designed to help children read and learn about the special characteristics and behaviors of the intriguing featured animals. Each book is an informative nonfiction companion to one of the colorful and charming fiction books in the *Animal Storybooks* series.

Each book in the *Let's Read About Animals* series is specially designed to support the young reader in the reading process. The familiar topics are appealing to young children and invite them to read — and reread — again and again. The full-color photographs and enhanced text further support the student during the reading process.

In addition to serving as wonderful picture books in schools, libraries, homes, and other places where children learn to love reading, these books are specifically intended to be read within an instructional guided reading group. This small group setting allows beginning readers to work with a fluent adult model as they make meaning from the text. After children develop fluency with the text and content, the books can be read independently. Children and adults alike will find these books supportive, engaging, and fun!

— Susan Nations, M.Ed., author/literacy coach/
consultant in literacy development

Look at those teeth! Now you see why **crocodiles** do not have many enemies.

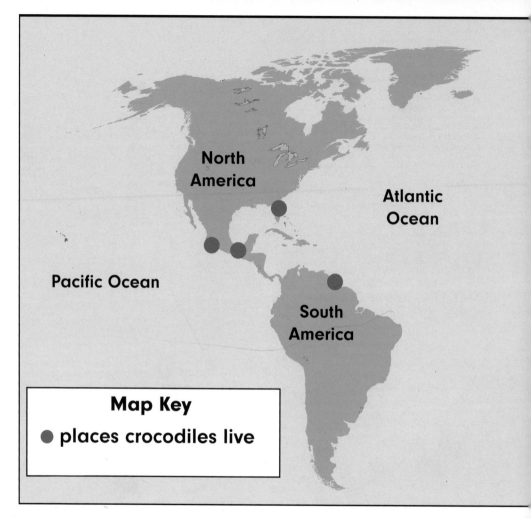

North
America

Atlantic
Ocean

Pacific Ocean

South
America

Map Key
● places crocodiles live

Fourteen kinds of crocodiles

live in the world.

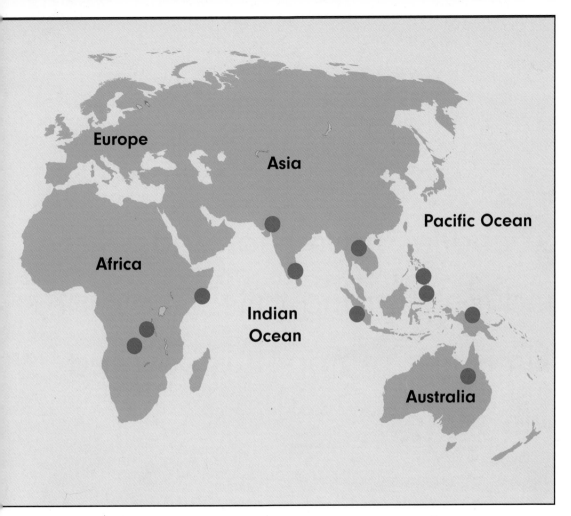

They live in warm, wet places.

The map shows where they live.

Crocodiles have short legs and long, strong tails. Their skin is like armor. It is covered with **scales**.

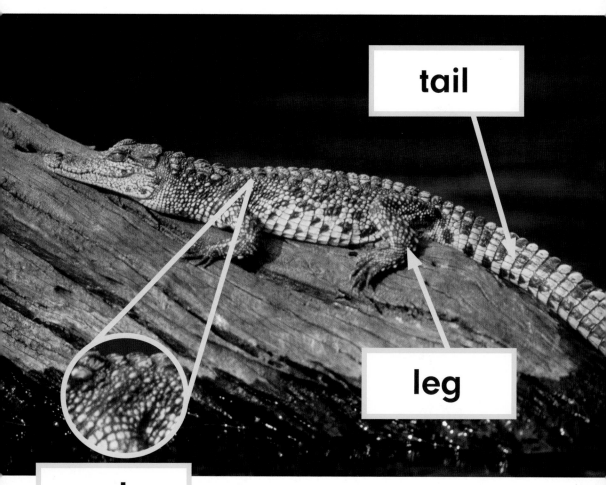

tail

leg

scales

Crocodiles like to lie in the Sun. They need the Sun to keep warm.

When they lie in the water, crocodiles look like bumpy logs! They are waiting for fish or other **prey** to come near.

Swish! A crocodile whips its tail back and forth to swim fast after its prey.

Snap! Its big jaws slam shut.
Gulp! A crocodile swallows
its prey without chewing.

jaw

A mother crocodile lays her eggs on land. She buries the eggs under leaves or in sand.

eggs

After the eggs hatch, the mother crocodile carries her babies to shallow water. She carries them in her mouth! Do you see her crocodile smile?

Glossary

armor — a hard, metal covering that soldiers used to protect their bodies in battles

crocodiles — large, lizardlike animals with sharp teeth and tough, scaly skin

enemies — animals that try to harm other animals

prey — animals that are hunted for food

scales — the hard, tough plates that cover and protect some animals and plants

shallow — not deep

For More Information

Books

The Cranky Crocodile. Animal Storybooks (series). Rebecca Johnson
  (Gareth Stevens)

The Crocodile. Life Cycles (series). Diana Noonan (Chelsea House)

Gator or Croc? Rookie Read-About Science (series). Allan Fowler
  (Children's Press)

Web Site

Creature Feature: Nile Crocodiles

www.nationalgeographic.com/kids/creature_feature/
  0107/crocodiles.html

Click to learn fun facts, watch a video, see a map
where Nile crocs live, and more.

Publisher's note to educators and parents: Our editors have carefully reviewed this
Web site to ensure that it is suitable for children. Many Web sites change frequently,
however, and we cannot guarantee that a site's future contents will continue to meet
our high standards of quality and educational value. Be advised that children should
be closely supervised whenever they access the Internet.

Index

About the Author

Kathleen Pohl has written and edited many children's books. Among them are animal tales, rhyming books, retold classics, and the forty-book series *Nature Close-Ups*. Most recently, she authored the Weekly Reader® Early Learning Library series *Where People Work*. She also served for many years as top editor of *Taste of Home* and *Country Woman* magazines. She and her husband, Bruce, live in the middle of beautiful Wisconsin woods and share their home with six goats, a llama, and all kinds of wonderful woodland creatures.